中英双语版
企鹅经典 名人大发现

克里斯托弗·哥伦布

[美] 邦尼·巴德（Bonnie Bader）◎著　[美] 南希·哈里森（Nancy Harrison）◎绘　周丽娟◎译

Who Was Christopher Columbus?

CNS 湖南科学技术出版社 小博集 BOOKY KIDS
·长沙·

著作权合同登记号：字18-2024-195

图书在版编目（CIP）数据

名人大发现．克里斯托弗·哥伦布 ：汉英对照 /（美）邦尼·巴德（Bonnie Bader）著 ；周丽娟译 ；（美）南希·哈里森（Nancy Harrison）绘．-- 长沙 ：湖南科学技术出版社，2025．1．--（企鹅经典）．
ISBN 978-7-5710-3270-8

Ⅰ．H319．4

中国国家版本馆CIP数据核字第2024RZ7725号

上架建议：科普读物

QI’E JINGDIAN · MINGREN DA FAXIAN：ZHONG-YING SHUANGYU BAN KELISITUOFU GELUNBU
企鹅经典 · 名人大发现：中英双语版　克里斯托弗 · 哥伦布

著　　者：［美］邦尼 · 巴德（Bonnie Bader）
绘　　者：［美］南希 · 哈里森（Nancy Harrison）
译　　者：周丽娟
出 版 人：潘晓山
责任编辑：刘　竞
策划出品：李　炜　张苗苗　文赛峰
策划编辑：马　瑄
特约编辑：杜佳美
营销编辑：付　佳　杨　朔　周晓茜
装帧设计：利　锐
内文排版：金锋工作室
出　　版：湖南科学技术出版社
（湖南省长沙市芙蓉中路416号　邮编：410008）
网　　址：www.hnstp.com
印　　刷：三河市航远印刷有限公司
经　　销：新华书店
开　　本：875 mm × 1230 mm 1/32
字　　数：101千字
印　　张：5
版　　次：2025年1月第1版
印　　次：2025年1月第1次印刷
书　　号：ISBN 978-7-5710-3270-8
定　　价：22.00元

若有质量问题，请致电质量监督电话：010-59096394　　团购电话：010-59320018

目　录

Contents

谁是克里斯托弗·哥伦布？

一个个子高高的男人在船甲板上来回踱步。自 1492 年 8 月 3 日起，他和他的船员已经在海上航行了七十天。他们从西班牙出发，已经航行了两千六百五十多英里[①]。现在，他们发现了陆地。克里斯托弗·哥伦布到达印度群岛的梦想是否终于实现了？

---

① 英里：英美制长度单位。1 英里≈ 1.609 千米。

多年来，哥伦布一直恳求葡萄牙和西班牙统治者出钱赞助这次航海之旅。他想向西航行，找到一条欧洲通往印度群岛的航线。印度群岛包括中国、日本和印度[①]。以前从来没有人这样做过。

1492年10月12日，太阳刚一升起，哥伦布和他的船员就登上岸边。哥伦布双膝跪地，亲吻着地面，哭泣起来。

① 此为15世纪前后欧洲国家对东亚、东南亚生产香料的岛屿的泛称，不是实指。

啊，前方将会有怎样的财富等着他！他将以英雄的身份回到西班牙。

但是哥伦布并不知道，这里不是印度群岛。那么他在哪里呢？哥伦布和他的船员在一块所有欧洲人都不知道的大陆上。克里斯托弗·哥伦布发现了一个新世界。

第一章

探险家的诞生

1451 年，一个名叫克里斯托福罗·科隆博的男孩在意大利城市热那亚出生。在英语世界里，他被称为克里斯托弗·哥伦布。

克里斯托弗的父亲是个羊毛纺织工，母亲是纺织工的女儿，也帮着家里做纺织活。家里人希望克里斯托弗

有朝一日能接管家里的生意。

但是年轻的克里斯托弗不愿意走父亲的老路。他喜欢大海，喜欢海上空气咸咸的味道，喜欢海风吹拂头发的感觉。热那亚是当时地中海地区一个繁忙的港口。克里斯托弗和弟弟巴尔托洛梅奥喜欢下到码头去。他们看着船只载着丝绸、茶叶、香料等来自东方的商品驶

入港口，又看着船只载着羊毛、铜、锡和武器驶离港口。克里斯托弗希望自己有一天能在那其中一只船上工作。

在那个时代，十岁男孩就能当船上侍者，跟随船只出海。船上侍者什么活都干——做饭，打扫卫生，拿取

工具和日常用品。克里斯托弗十四岁时，获得了他在船上的第一份工作。

克里斯托弗把时间分别花在帮助父亲和海上航行上。他航行到爱尔兰和冰岛等地，学习了大量在辽阔海域驾驶船只的技术。这些技术在他今后的人生中将起到非常重要的作用。

克里斯托弗十九岁时长成了一个强壮有力的小伙子。没人确切知道他当时长什么样。有人说他身材高大，肩膀宽阔。据说他皮肤白皙，长着红色的头发和淡蓝色的眼睛，不仅身体强健还思维敏捷。也有人说他太过固执，脾气不好，但是又对自己非常自信。他一旦下定决心做什么事，就绝不会放弃。有一件事情克里斯托弗·哥伦布非常确定——他想成为一位出名的海船船长，既声名远播又多产富有。

第二章

绘制世界地图

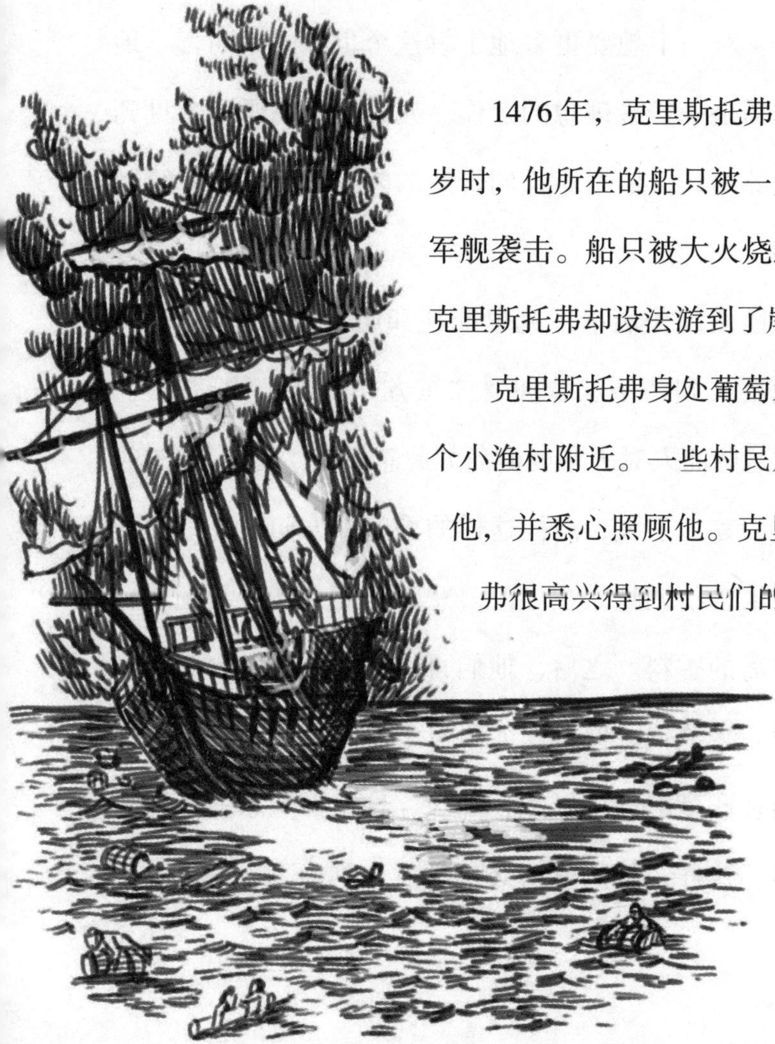

1476年，克里斯托弗二十五岁时，他所在的船只被一只法国军舰袭击。船只被大火烧毁，但克里斯托弗却设法游到了岸上。

克里斯托弗身处葡萄牙的一个小渔村附近。一些村民发现了他，并悉心照顾他。克里斯托弗很高兴得到村民们的帮助。

但是，他不想待在一个僻静的村庄里。他很快就去了首都里斯本。

克里斯托弗在里斯本住了九年。他的弟弟巴尔托洛梅奥也住在这里，他们一起开了一家店，当起了地图制作师。对一个想要更多地了解这个世界的人而言，地图制作师是一份最理想的工作。兄弟俩会在码头会见到港船只的船长，根据船长们告知的内容收集信息并绘制地图。

在地图制作店里，克里斯托弗听到商人们的议论。他们想要找到一条从欧洲通往东方印度群岛的新航线。为什么这些商人对去印度群岛如此感兴趣？答案是香料，像胡椒、姜、丁香、肉桂这样的香料。人们在烹饪中使用香料给食物调味。在埃及，意大利商人能够买到来自印度群岛的香料。之后，他们再将香料转手卖给整个欧洲，赚一大笔钱。但是，如果有个探险家能够找到一条直接通往印度群岛的航线，那么，这个探险家就能够买到香料。这样，他们就不必依靠意大利商人。所以，谁能够找到一条通往印度群岛的航线，谁就能通过香料贸易发财。

在那个时候，大部分人都知道地球是圆的。但是，他们不知道的是地球到底有多大。人们认为世界只有一块大陆——欧洲、亚洲和非洲——被一片叫“大洋”的水体包围着。

在那个时候，那些到过印度群岛的旅行者走的都是陆路。探险家马可·波罗写的《马可·波罗游记》讲述了他从意大利到中国的旅行。哥伦布读了这本书，他对马可·波罗在书中描写的像人的拳头一样大的红宝石和由黄金铺地的宫殿非常着迷。

哥伦布下定决心要成为首个全程通过航海抵达印度群岛的人。葡萄牙国王曾试图派遣船只绕过非洲，向东航行，前往印度群岛。但这些船只都不断折返。船员们说这条航线太长，他们不知道会驶向哪里。可是哥伦布有了另外一个想法。他认为这个想法更好。他要向西航行去印度群岛。他要直接跨越大洋航海！

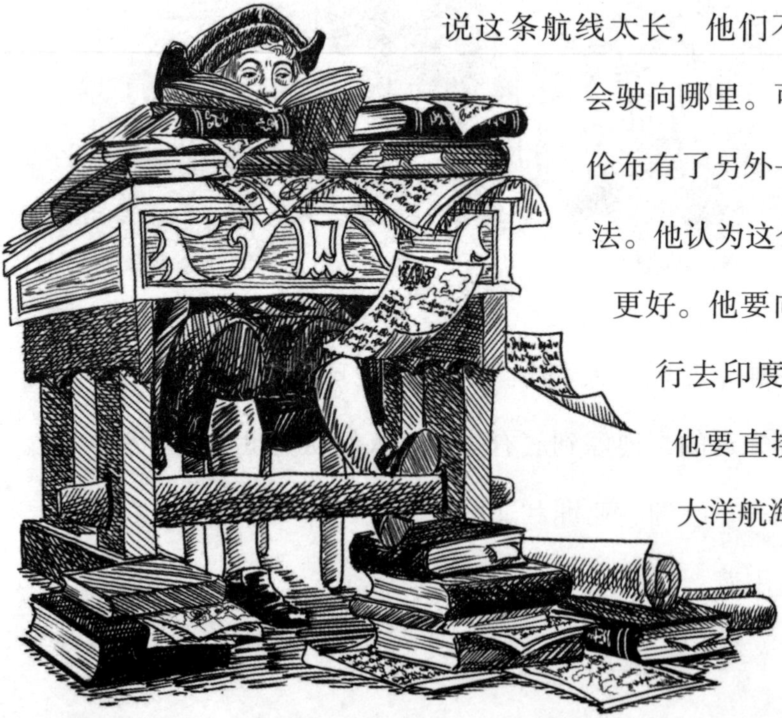

其他人嘲笑哥伦布的计划。穿越“大洋”？为什么？那得花上好几个月！哥伦布带不了那么多食物和水，他和船员要怎么活下去？

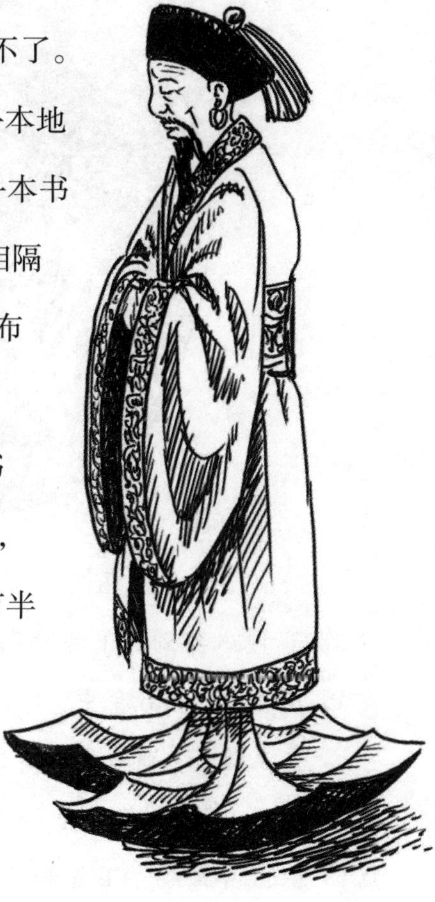

这些问题，哥伦布回答不了。于是他翻阅更多书，一本接一本地阅读有关世界旅行的书。有一本书说加那利群岛和日本之间只相隔三千海里[①]。而日本正是哥伦布想去的印度群岛的一个地区。

另一本关于印度群岛的书说，那里有长着伞状脚的人，有肩膀上长着眼睛的人，还有半狮半鹰的动物！大多数人认为这些故事是杜撰出来的。不过，哥伦布阅读得

① 海里：计量海洋上距离的长度单位。1 海里≈ 1.852 千米。

马可·波罗和丝绸之路

1271 年，马可·波罗随其父、叔去东方，于 1275 年到达上都，见到了统治者忽必烈可汗。在之后的两百年中，印度、中国和欧洲的贸易一直在增长。商人们沿着这条名为“丝绸之路”的陆路行走，对丝绸、珍珠、黄金、红宝石、胡椒、肉豆蔻、丁香和茶叶等商品进行交易。但是，这条道路既漫长又危险。旅行者们必须穿越沙漠和山脉，路上还有强盗等着抢劫他们的货物。到了 15 世纪，欧洲人迫切希望找到另外一条通往印度群岛的路线。

越多，就变得越兴奋。

对克里斯托弗·哥伦布而言，更重要的是，他相信是上帝有意要他踏上去印度群岛的航海之旅。上帝让他喜欢大海，上帝把他带到葡萄牙。那么，在航海旅程中，上帝将会为他指引方向。

第三章

再三等待

克里斯托弗需要有人出钱赞助他航海。这个人既要富有又要有权势，就像葡萄牙国王那样的人。但是，哥伦布如何才能见到国王呢？他需要有个门路，有个联系途径。

1478 年，克里斯托弗 · 哥伦布娶了费莉帕 · 佩雷斯特

葡萄牙国王若奥二世

雷洛·莫尼斯。她的家族在王宫里有朋友。

但是直到1484年，克里斯托弗·哥伦布才最终见到了葡萄牙国王若奥二世。哥伦布站在国王面前，个子很高。他告诉国王他知道通往印度群岛的正确路线，并对这条路线很有把握。哥伦布还承诺他将带回许多黄金。若奥国王听他侃侃而谈。可国王说了什么吗？

国王说“不”。

克里斯托弗·哥伦布并不气馁。如果葡萄牙国王不支持他，也许西班牙的斐迪南国王和伊莎贝拉女王[①]会支持他。

克里斯托弗等待拜见若奥国王的时候，他的妻子已经去世。因此，他前往西班牙时，把他们年幼的儿子迭戈交给一个修道院里的修道士来照顾。一个年幼的男孩是无法在危险重重的跨海航行中存活下来的。

想要见到伊莎贝拉女王和斐迪南国王，哥伦布必须等待九个月。为什么？那时候，西班牙王廷从一个城市

① 当时西班牙双王当政。伊莎贝拉继承了王位，后与西班牙另一地区的另一位国王斐迪南结婚，他们共同执掌西班牙。

搬迁到另一个城市。哥伦布负担不起追随王室的费用。因此，他在科尔多瓦城居住下来等待。在这里，他遇到一个名叫比阿特丽斯·恩里克斯·德哈拉纳的年轻乡村姑娘。两年后比阿特丽斯生下了哥伦布的第二个儿子，一个名叫斐迪南的男孩。

1486 年 5 月 1 日，哥伦布终于见到了斐迪南国王和伊莎贝拉女王。他希望国王和女王会同意这次航海之旅。

他们会看到哥伦布是个多么出色的基督徒。他会将基督教信仰传遍新的大地。此外，他的航海之旅也会让西班牙变得非常富有。

但当时西班牙正在打一场劳民伤财的战争。国家没有钱来支持一场前往印度群岛的远洋航行。哥伦布不得不等待。还要再等待？哦，不！

两年过去了。哥伦布再次试图寻求葡萄牙国王若奥二世的出资赞助。但是若奥二世太忙了——他忙着庆祝另一个探险家巴塞洛缪·迪亚士的归来。哥伦布向西航行的计划在若奥国王看来仍然是荒唐愚蠢的。

于是哥伦布只好返回西班牙。斐迪南和伊莎贝拉正在打的这场战争持续了三年。这三年，哥伦布一直在等待。等他回去再见国王和女王时，他终于得到了期待已久的答复。

同意！

哥伦布此时四十一岁，要踏上这样一场艰辛的旅程，年纪已经有点大了。

巴塞洛缪·迪亚士

巴塞洛缪·迪亚士

葡萄牙国王若奥二世急于找到一条通往印度群岛的贸易路线，于是派遣巴塞洛缪·迪亚士出海航行。1487 年 8 月，迪亚士离开里斯本。尽管天气恶劣，但他和他的船员意识到绕过非洲南端航行可能行得通。他们把非洲南端称为风暴角，因为他们在那里遭遇了可怕的天气。（风暴角后来改名为好望角。）1488 年，迪亚士回到葡萄牙，成为英雄。虽然迪亚士没有绕过非洲南端一直航行下去（1497 年瓦斯科·达·伽马做到了这一点），但是迪亚士因为帮助开辟一条通往东方的新贸易路线而受到人们的赞誉。

对长年的等待，哥伦布感到很气愤，因此他提出了一些要求。

他想要得到什么？如果他取得成功，他希望得到海军上将的头衔。他希望掌管所有他发现的领土。他还希望保有自己在那些领土上发现的财宝的十分之一。

伊莎贝拉女王简直不敢相信自己所听到的话。这个傲慢的家伙是谁？她可不会对他的要求妥协。是的，伊莎贝拉女王和克里斯托弗·哥伦布断绝了来往。

那么，克里斯托弗·哥伦布又是怎么做的呢？他收拾好行李，套上骡子，去见法国国王。也许法国国王会派哥伦布出海航行。

哥伦布启程出发时，听到身后传来了马蹄声。那是伊莎贝拉女王的人。她改变主意了。她可不想让法国国王得到有可能属于她的财富。而且，如果哥伦布失败，她也不会有任何损失，她和法国国王都得不到任何东西。伊莎贝拉女王和哥伦布签下了一份协议。

哥伦布的航海之旅即将开始。

第四章

海上航行

现在，克里斯托弗·哥伦布需要船只和船员。伊莎贝拉女王命令帕洛斯镇的人给哥伦布造两只船。帕洛斯在战争中支持了女王的敌人，因此她要惩罚这个小镇。

当时造船费用非常昂贵，但是镇上的人必须服从女王。

帕洛斯造的两只船被命名为“尼娜”号和“平塔”号。它们是卡拉维尔帆船，小但是速度很快。但是哥伦布还想得到更大的船。他找啊找啊，能找到的最大的一只船是六十英尺[①]长的“圣玛丽亚”号，那是一只速度缓慢的货船。但他仍决定凑合使用这只船。

① 英尺：英美制长度单位。1 英尺≈ 0.305 米。

卡瑞克帆船和卡拉维尔帆船

卡瑞克帆船

卡瑞克帆船（西班牙语中这个词和英语的“现在”一词同音）和卡拉维尔帆船是两种能够远距离航行的船。卡瑞克帆船是一种庞大沉重，速度缓慢，配有三或四根桅杆的船。它非常适合运输货物，也能在波涛汹涌的海面保持稳定。它还有很大的空间，因此能为远洋航行储备大量的食物和水。卡拉维尔帆船是一种新型船。它有一到三根桅杆，重量比卡瑞克帆船更轻。

卡拉维尔帆船

来自帕洛斯的两兄弟，马丁·平松和比森特·平松签订协议担任船长。马丁将指挥“平塔”号，比森特将指挥“尼娜”号。哥伦布则将担任“圣玛丽亚”号的船长，他还负责掌管整个船队。

他们很难找到心甘情愿去的船员。大多数人认为哥伦布向西航行的想法既荒谬又愚蠢。

哥伦布求三拜四，东央西浼，甚至用上了威胁的手段，终于找到大约九十个人加入他的队伍。许多人是平松兄弟的朋友和亲戚，别的则是一些犯人。他们从监狱里被释放出来随哥伦布一道航海。他们中的二十四人搭乘“尼娜”号，二十六人搭乘“平塔”号，四十人搭乘“圣玛丽亚”号。

他们大部分人做水手。但也有人负责修理船只，有人负责钓鱼，有人负责清洁打扫，还有人负责制作木桶。哥伦布还带了一个助理和一个医生。船上没有女人。（在那个年代，女人不做水手。）

船上装满了补给品，有绳索、地图和指南针；有鲜

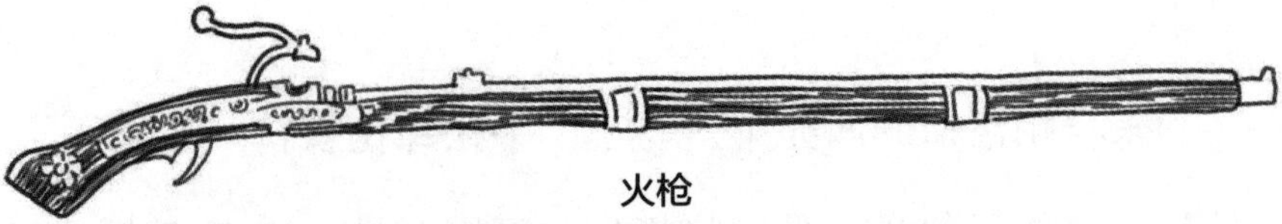

火枪

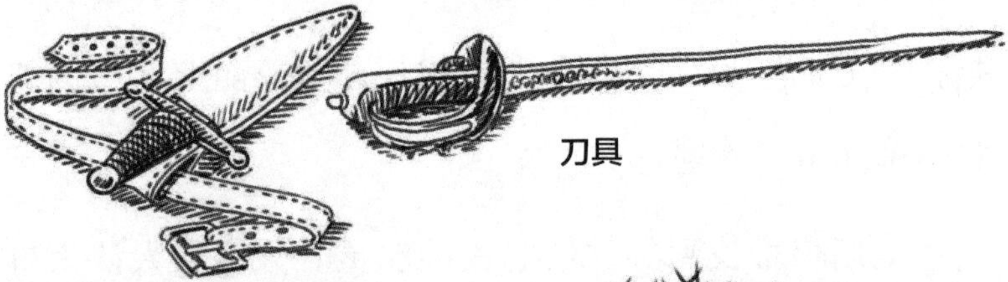

刀具

沙丁鱼

鸡蛋

鲜奶

水果

肉、干肉、鲜奶、水果、鸡蛋、沙丁鱼、凤尾鱼、橄榄油、葡萄干、饼干、奶酪、豌豆、大蒜、洋葱、大米和豆子；还有许多桶水。他们携带了大炮、弩和火枪，以

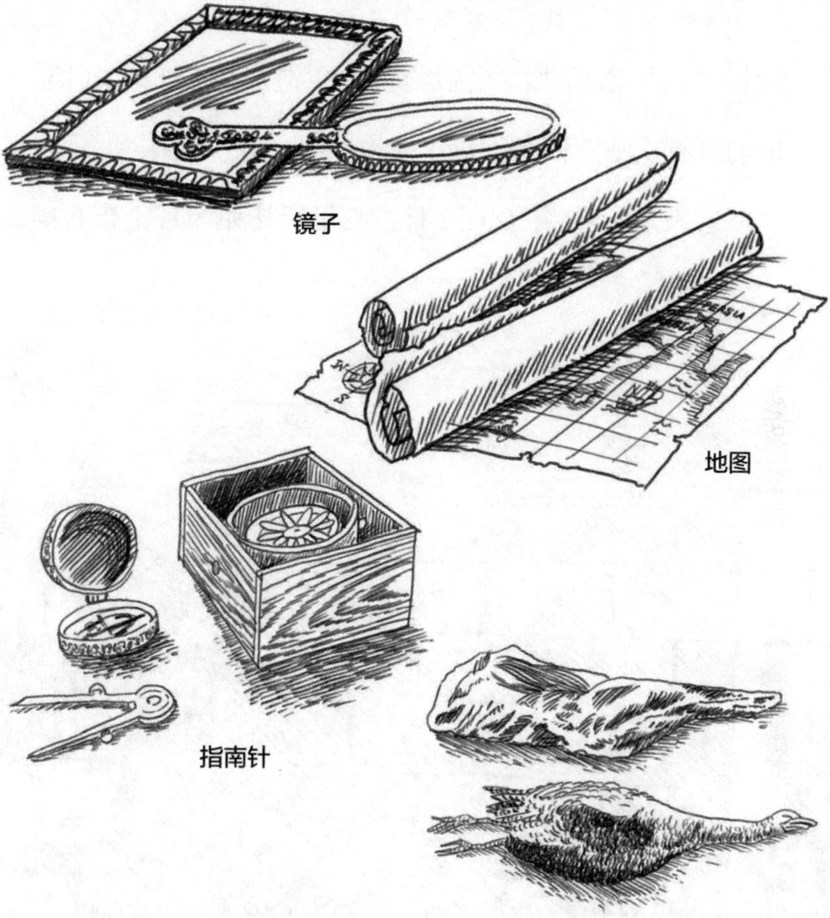

防和敌对船只发生冲突。为了进行贸易，他们还带了铃铛、剪刀、刀具、硬币、串珠和镜子。

如果哥伦布期待人们为他办一场离别欢送会，那他就错了。帕洛斯人对出钱给哥伦布造船感到非常气愤。他们没有欢呼，而是发出了嘘声。

这天是1492年8月2日。克里斯托弗·哥伦布召集

他的船员来到海边祈祷。他们祈求航行一路平安，祈求他们能发现新领土，找到新财富。

接着，1492年8月3日清晨，“尼娜”号、“平塔”号和“圣玛丽亚”号从帕洛斯扬帆起航了。哥伦布的计划是向南航行至加那利群岛。在那里，他将掉转船头，向西航行，前往西邦戈（今天的日本）。哥伦布认为加那利群岛通往西邦戈的航线是一条直线，他只要从加那利群岛向西航行二千四百英里就能到达印度群岛。这是他的计划，但是他的计划错了。

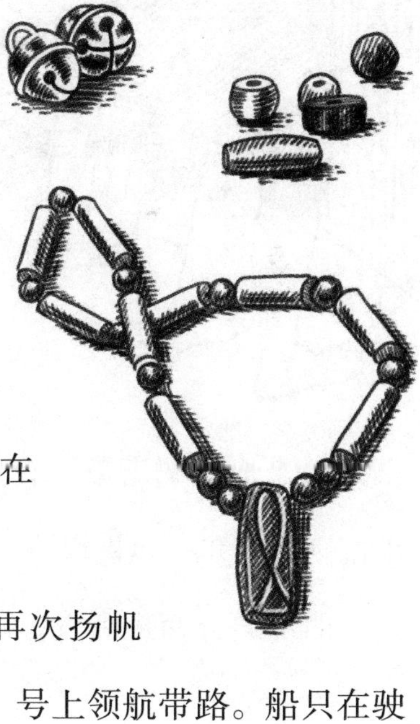

三只船在加那利群岛抛锚停泊。哥伦布和马丁·平松上岸购买更多的商品——玻璃串珠、黄铜铃铛、颜色鲜艳的布匹、珠宝和镜子。这些商品能够在印度群岛用来交换新鲜食物。

1492年9月6日，他们再次扬帆起航。哥伦布在“圣玛丽亚”号上领航带路。船只在驶入开阔海域的头几天，航行得一帆风顺。船员们看上去

很高兴。他们唱着歌，在船的两侧钓起鱼来。日落时，他们则聚集在一起祈祷。

船员们分两班睡觉。一班人白天工作，另一班人晚上工作。

但随着日子一天天过去，船员们变得焦躁不安起来。

他们在海上航行了很长时间。他们到底走了多远？哥伦布有两本航海日志。在一本日志里，他记录了每天航行的真实距离。而在另一本日志里——这本日志他的船员可以翻看，他记录的航行英里数更少。据哥伦布说，他不想让船员们觉得路程太远而受到惊吓。

但船员们还是被吓到了。他们驶入了大洋的中心。他们能发现什么？他们还能回家吗？于是，哥伦布跟船员们不停地说所有的财富在等待着他们。

船员们留意着任何陆地的迹象，留意着任何能给他们带来希望的东西。比如海面上的一点海草，一群飞翔的鸟。

9 月 25 日，马丁 · 平松觉得他看到了陆地。但其实不是，他没有看到。

船只又继续航行了两个多礼拜。大多数船员从来没有航行过这么长时间。对他们来说，这几个礼拜似乎永远没有尽头。

而且船上的生活并不令人舒心愉悦。哥伦布的船员们既不洗澡也不刷牙。他们光着脚在甲板上走路，有时会踩到一只虫子或者一坨老鼠屎。当他们要上厕所时，怎么办呢？他们就来到船舷边解决问题！

每只船上只有一个船舱，是给船长用的。其余船员

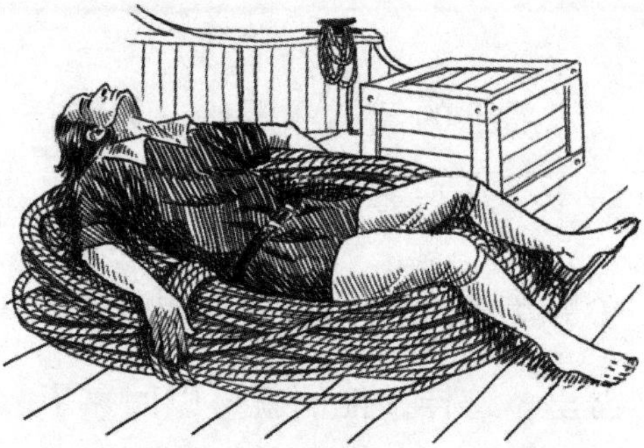

能在哪里找到干燥地方就睡在哪里——睡在一圈绳索上或者一个木桶旁。

船上没有厨师。船员们只能自己做吃的。但是首先，他们还得和那些想争夺食物的老鼠战斗！有时候，他们钓了鱼，再把鱼用盐腌制，然后晒干。如果船员们想吃饼干，他们得先把虫子从面粉里挑出来。大多数时候，食物是腐坏变质或者味道不好的。因此，他们在食物里加入大量大蒜来掩盖难吃的味道。而且，他们通常在晚上用餐，这样他们就看不见食物里有什么东西在爬来爬去了！

船上很脏。老鼠在木板上跑来跑去。到处都有跳蚤，还有虱子。所有人身上都长了虱子！

船上的气氛一天比一天糟糕。有些船员认为哥伦布疯了。他们看见他在甲板上走来走去，盯着天空看。这个疯子要把他们带到哪里去？有的人都想把哥伦布扔进海里，这样，他们就可以回家了。

10 月 7 日，他们又一次以为看到了陆地。哥伦布这时承诺，如果三天之内不能抵达陆地，他就掉转船队返航回家。

幸运的是，10 月 10 日这天晚上，哥伦布觉得他看到了陆地。

这次是真的。10 月 12 日午夜刚过，“平塔”号上一个船员大声喊道：“陆地！陆地！”

是的，他们可以看到陆地隐隐约约的轮廓。大家都欣喜万分。他们抵达了印度群岛，或者说他们是这么认为的。

第五章

瞧，陆地！

10 月 12 日，太阳刚刚升起，哥伦布就准备登陆上岸。他和他的军官穿上最好的衣服，挤上小划艇。他们带了一面西班牙国旗和一些用来交易的商品，还带了刀和剑，以防遇到不友好的当地人。

他们即将找到什么财富？黄金？香料？

哥伦布踏上了这片陌生的土地。他双膝跪地，亲吻着地面，感谢上帝指引他来到这里。他插上国旗，宣称这块土地属于西班牙，并给它取名为“圣萨尔瓦多”。

岛上一些土著居民在灌木丛后面注视着哥伦布。这些人被称为泰诺人。泰诺人慢慢靠近。哥伦布和手下盯着这些奇怪的人看。这些人既没佩戴黄金首饰，也没穿丝绸衣服。实际上，他们几乎什么也没穿。

这些土著人也同样感到惊讶。泰诺人从来没有见过白人，也从来没有见过穿着衣服或是留着胡子的人。还有那些行驶在海里的船！多么奇怪！

泰诺人

泰诺人由一位酋长统治。酋长可以是男人也可以是女人。他们家家户户住在由木杆、稻草编制物和树叶制成的房子里。泰诺人是出色的农夫、渔夫和猎人，也是技艺娴熟的木雕师。他们还能用棉花编织出美丽的吊床。泰诺人崇拜各种不同的神。哥伦布相信自己的使命是使他们全部皈依基督教。在哥伦布到达这里之前，泰诺人过着幸福和平的生活。但欧洲人带来了天花、麻疹和流感等疾病。在之后的三十年里，有百分之八十到百分之九十的泰诺人死去了。

哥伦布认为这个岛离印度群岛海岸不远。于是他把遇到的这些人称为“印第安人”。当然，这个岛离印度群岛绝对不近。哥伦布的船实际上是在今天的巴哈马群岛登陆的。圣萨尔瓦多岛风景优美。这里有郁郁葱葱的树木、蜿蜒曲折的河流和波光粼粼的大湖。

泰诺人给了西班牙人棉花、木制长矛和鹦鹉。那是许多五颜六色，叽叽喳喳的鹦鹉。作为回报，泰诺人得到了玻璃串珠和铃铛。

为什么寻找黄金?

黄金一直都很珍贵，因为它非常稀有、美丽。1370 年到 1420 年之间，欧洲许多大金矿都开采光了。因此，欧洲的商人们开始前往非洲和亚洲寻找黄金。寻找黄金的竞争非常激烈。后来，1511 年（哥伦布去世之后），斐迪南国王宣布：“尽量人道地拿到黄金，但如果不能，要不惜一切代价得到黄金!”在很短一段时间内，中美洲盛产黄金的印加文明和阿兹特克文明被西班牙征服者摧毁了。

但是，铺着黄金地板的宫殿在哪里？一切的财富和香料又在哪里？哥伦布看到一些泰诺人鼻子上佩戴着小金环。他推断着，这里的某个地方一定有黄金。

哥伦布尝试用手势和姿势进行交流。他挥舞着手臂，寻问哪里有黄金。

土著人用手势告诉他，南边有个岛屿有黄金。哥伦布心想，那里一定是中国。

10 月 14 日，哥伦布和他的船员出发了。但是，他们在起锚之前，绑架了几个泰诺人，将他们带上了船。他们会教这些泰诺人西班牙语，好让这些泰诺人在其他岛上为他们充当翻译。

“尼娜”号、“平塔”号和“圣玛丽亚”号花了两个礼拜的时间在不同岛屿之间航行。他们遇到了许多热情友好的土著人。土著人给了他们许多棉花、长矛和鹦鹉，但是没有黄金。

哥伦布向印第安人请求帮助。印第安人示意他向南航行，去另一座岛屿。哥伦布以为他们说的是日本。10 月 28 日，“尼娜”号、“平塔”号和“圣玛丽亚”号抵达

了这座岛屿。当哥伦布看见当地人手腕和脚踝上都戴着黄金饰物时，他非常激动。哥伦布断定，这不是日本，这是中国！更好了！

哥伦布又一次错了。实际上他在古巴。哥伦布派遣一批人去向中国那位著名的统治者大可汗介绍自己。当然，这批人回去时，并没有带回大可汗的任何音信。更糟糕的是，这里没有黄金。到了向前航行的时候了。

第六章

船只失事

到12月初，“平塔”号已经独自外出去寻找黄金了。天气逐渐变冷，暴风雨也越来越多了。如果“尼娜”号和“圣玛丽亚”号想要在冬天来临之前回到西班牙，他们必须马上离开。

但是，哥伦布认为还有许多地方没有探索，因此他命令船队继续前行。12月6日，哥伦布将他们登陆的那个岛屿命名为伊斯帕尼奥拉岛，因为这里的树木让他想起了西班牙。

后来，在平安夜，灾难降临了。一些船员在欢庆节日。哥伦布在度过一个漫长的夜晚之后睡着了。“圣玛丽亚”号上的大多数船员也睡着了，只留下一个船上的男孩负责照看船只。

风很平静，船缓慢向前行驶。然而在午夜过后的某个时刻，“圣玛丽亚”号撞上了一座珊瑚礁。一声叫喊传来，哥伦布被惊醒了。他竭尽全力想挽救这只船。但为时已晚，船体两侧已经开裂了。

“圣玛丽亚”号正在沉没！

哥伦布请求援助。当地的泰诺人酋长派人划独木舟赶来。他们将“圣玛丽亚”号上的货物卸下来，把贸易物品和补给物品转移到岸上。

这些土著人除了帮忙卸船上的货物，还带来了黄金！数量不多，只有一些样品——面具、珠宝首饰，还有其他小饰品。

哥伦布损失了一只船，等他从这种震惊中恢复过来，他意识到“圣玛丽亚”号的沉没是一个征兆。上帝想让他在这个岛屿登陆。毕竟，那位酋长给了他戒指、项链和用黄金制作的面具。而黄金是他来这里的目的！也许现在，他们可以回家了。

但是，哥伦布只剩下一只船了。马丁·平松和“平

塔”号仍然下落不明。他们不能所有人都乘坐小型“尼娜”号返回西班牙。于是，哥伦布修建了一座堡垒。四十个人会留在这里过冬。这四十个人将寻找黄金。等哥伦布回来的时候，他会带着他们（和黄金）回家。

哥伦布利用“圣玛丽亚”号上的木材修建堡垒。他们在堡垒四周挖了一条壕沟，还架上“圣玛丽亚”号上的大炮。哥伦布将堡垒命名为拉纳维达堡，是西班牙语“圣诞节”的意思。

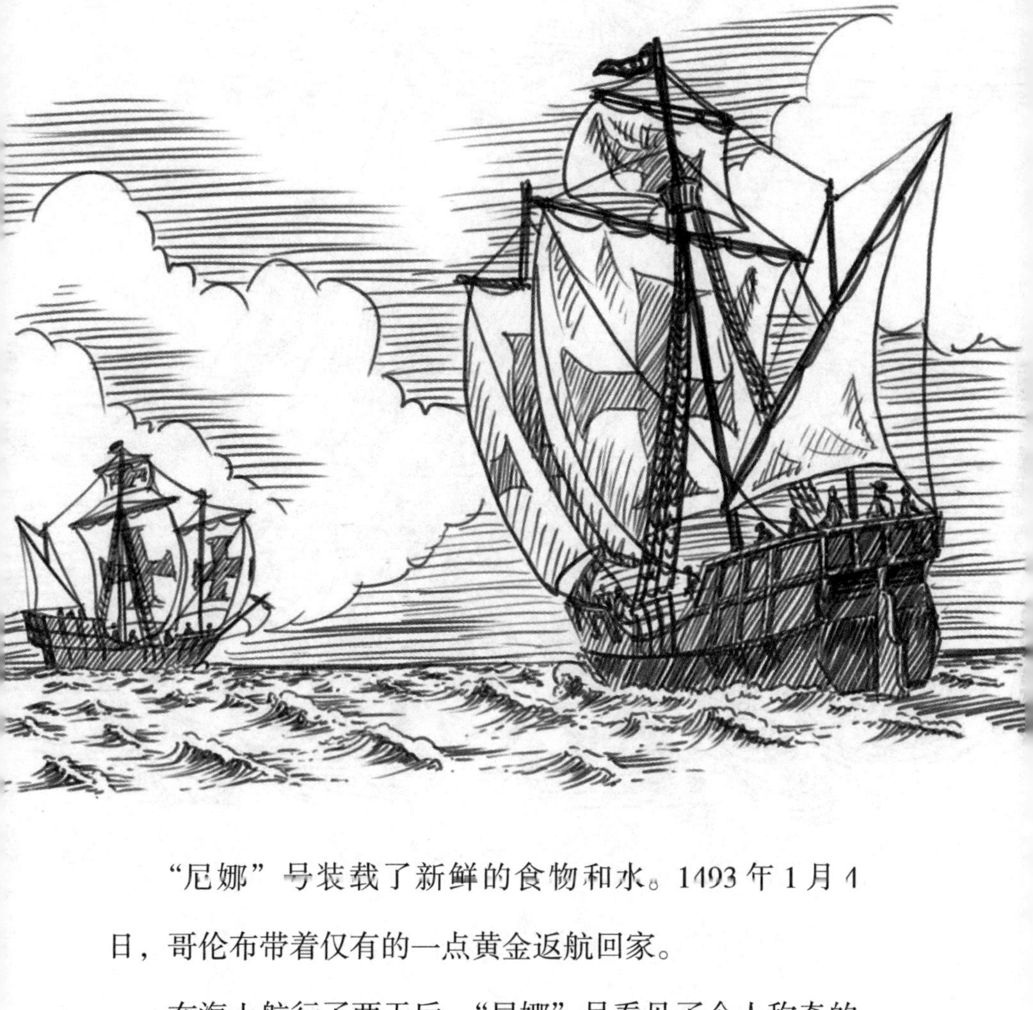

“尼娜”号装载了新鲜的食物和水。1493 年 1 月 4 日，哥伦布带着仅有的一点黄金返航回家。

在海上航行了两天后，“尼娜”号看见了令人称奇的景象。是“平塔”号！两只船相遇了，它们一同继续返航回家，直到一场可怕的暴风雨把它们再次分开。

哥伦布担心“平塔”号会永远消失不见。暴风雨越来越猛烈。如果他们都淹死了怎么办？那就没人知道他的航海已经成功了。于是，哥伦布抓起一张羊皮纸，将他发现新陆地的事写了下来。他用布包裹好这封信，在

布的外面封上一层蜡，然后将整个东西放进一个木桶里。他希望有一天，有人会发现木桶，并读到哥伦布所取得的成就。

暴风雨肆虐了十五天。尽管如此，哥伦布还是继续向前航行。毕竟，他能有什么选择呢？

3 月 15 日，哥伦布在帕洛斯海域抛锚停泊。从他上次见到这个美丽的海港起，已经差不多有七个半月了。他当时一定很高兴。而且，令人称奇的是，“平塔”号也平安归来了。

当然，斐迪南国王和伊莎贝拉女王想要立即见到哥伦布。于是，哥伦布启程前往巴塞罗那。所到之处，人们纷纷跑上街道，想要一睹哥伦布和他的船员的风采。人们之前从来没有见过印第安人、鹦鹉或是玉米。

最后，哥伦布到达王宫。斐迪南国王和伊莎贝拉女

王坐在一顶金色的华盖下面。当哥伦布向国王和女王走去时，这对王室夫妇站了起来。只有大贵族才会受到这样的欢迎。哥伦布亲吻他们的手背，在他们身旁坐下。接着，哥伦布讲述了自己的旅程。他展示了自己带回来的财宝。有五颜六色的鹦鹉，有黄金鼻环。当然黄金不是很多，但还是有一些的。他还带来了玉米、番薯和丝兰。现在，没有人嘲笑克里斯托弗·哥伦布了。

最重要的是，国王和女王信守承诺。哥伦布被授予了海军上将头衔，并被任命为总督，掌管他发现的所有领土。并且，他还得到了他带回的所有财产的十分之一。

克里斯托弗·哥伦布成了英雄。他与国王肩并肩，骑着马穿过巴塞罗那城。人们欢呼喝彩。这是他一生中最辉煌的时刻。

很快，他的光辉岁月就要结束了。

第七章
再次航海

哥伦布接到进行第二次航海的命令。他将返回伊斯帕尼奥拉岛，带回留在那里的船员，并留下更多人在那片土地上建立殖民地。

哥伦布非常高兴。这又是一个带黄金回来的好机会。

第一次航海时，哥伦布实际上不得不求人加入他的船队。这一次，大约有一千二百至一千五百人自告奋勇、着急忙慌地加入进来。谁知道这次航海又会找到什么财富呢？

目前的船员包括牧师（为了让当地人皈依基督教）、贵族、农民和其他有熟练技术的工人。就连哥伦布的弟弟迭戈也签了协议加入进来了。

哥伦布得到了十七只船。“尼娜”号是其中一只。哥伦布指挥一只以失事船只命名的船“圣玛丽亚”号。

这些船只载满了食物和水。这一次，他们带上了马匹，以供他们登陆后使用，还带了用于农场养殖的羊、

猪和用于种植的小麦和大麦种子。

1493 年 9 月 25 日，船队从加的斯港启航。这一次，

跨洋航行更加容易，因为哥伦布知道航线。这回没人抱怨了。

哥伦布第二次航海发现的岛屿

在返回伊斯帕尼奥拉岛的途中，哥伦布和他的船员在许多岛屿上停留过。多米尼加岛是他们到达的第一个岛屿。哥伦布将其命名为“多米尼加”，因为它是在一个礼拜日（1943 年 11 月 3 日）被发现的。在瓜德罗普岛，哥伦布和他的船员第一次尝到了菠萝的味道。圣玛丽亚·拉雷东达岛就是那个“圆形岛屿”。哥伦布还发现了维尔京群岛和波多黎各岛。

哥伦布发现了新岛屿。他发现了棉花、更多五颜六色的鹦鹉、水果。啊，他还发现了美丽的风景！苍翠的群山，开阔的峡谷，波光粼粼的河流和有白色泡沫的瀑布。但他们也看到了可怕的事情。女人被抓起来当奴隶，一些人吃人（他们被称为食人族）。哥伦布和他的船员没有在这些岛屿上停留很久。

1493 年 11 月 27 日晚，船队抵达伊斯帕尼奥拉岛。其中一只船立即发射了一枚炮弹。岸上没有人回应。留在岛上的人去哪里了？他们发生了什么事？哥伦布和他的船员被吓到了。

突然，他们听到船桨拍打水面的声音。会不会是哥伦布的船员来了？不是，那是一只载满泰诺人的独木舟。泰诺人带来了可怕的消息。堡垒被烧毁了，所有西班牙人都死了。发生了什么事？目前尚不清楚。有人说是西班牙人自己打了起来，他们自相残杀。有人说这些定居者生了病，死掉了。还有人说是附近的一个部落杀了这些西班牙人，烧毁了他们的居住点。不管真相如何，拉

纳维达堡已经不存在了。一个新的定居点必须重新建立起来。

在一个炎热的没有干净水源的沼泽地区，哥伦布和他的船员开始建立一个新的殖民地。为向女王表示敬意，他们给这个殖民地取名为“伊莎贝拉”。但是他们选择的地点很差。这里的蚊虫成群结队地围着他们叮咬。

人们很不高兴。这可不是他们航海来这里的目的。他们想要的是黄金。更糟糕的是，许多人病倒了。他们生病，也许是因为被蚊虫叮咬，也许是因为没有足够可吃的食物，他们种的庄稼长势不好，又或者只是因为他

们太累了。

他们别无选择，只得派一部分船只返回西班牙，去拿食物和药物。于是，1494 年 2 月 2 日，十二只船只返航回家。

哥伦布留了下来。为什么？强烈的寻找黄金的愿望让他留了下来。他派出多批身体健康的人去寻找黄金。但每一次，他们都空手而归。他们发现河床里到处都是小金粒，但这些小金粒不足以让国王和女王满意。

哥伦布听说有个叫希巴欧的地方有储量丰富的采金区。于是他让迭戈管理伊莎贝拉地区，自己启程。他找到了一些黄金，但和之前一样，数量不多。

马可·波罗所描述的岛屿西邦戈在哪里？哥伦布第一次开始担心起来。

哥伦布带领三只船驶回古巴以及他曾去过的其他岛屿。1494 年 9 月底，当哥伦布回到伊斯帕尼奥拉岛时，他病得很严重。但他仍然没有找到多少黄金。

回到伊莎贝拉地区，蚊子似乎变得更大个了。他的船员也病得更厉害，而且情绪也更加激愤。泰诺人的情况也变得更糟糕。哥伦布要求泰诺人为他寻找黄金。每

个成年泰诺人必须给他提供一定数量的黄金，否则就要面临严厉的惩罚。

泰诺人试图反击。然而他们的简易剑器和弓、箭不是西班牙人武器的对手。西班牙人拥有弩和火枪。

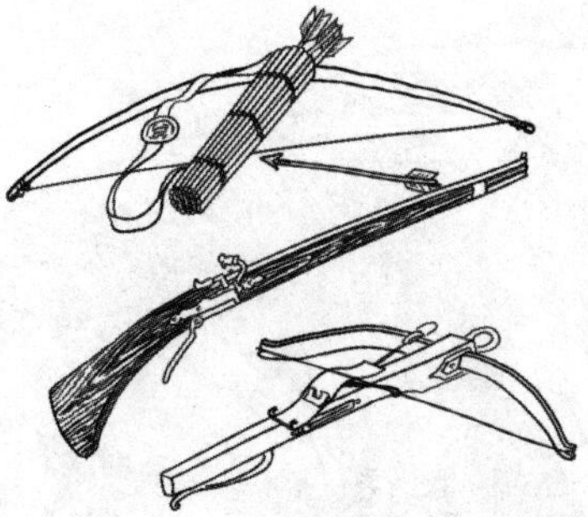

因为拿不出黄金给斐迪南国王和伊莎贝拉女王，哥伦布决定带一些泰诺人回西班牙做奴隶。这是一件可怕的事情。但是，哥伦布觉得这是他的权利。毕竟，他宣称过这片土地属于西班牙。因此，拥有这片土地上的人不也是他的权利吗？答案当然是否定的——这不是他的权利。尽管如此，哥伦布还是把五百名泰诺人带上船，把他们运送到西班牙。也许奴隶可以在市场上出售，给他们赚到钱。

哥伦布也感到忧心焦虑，因为他知道有消息传回了斐迪南国王和伊莎贝拉女王那里，说他不是一个好统帅，说他既固执又傲慢。

哥伦布决定他必须返回西班牙替自己辩护。出现的所有问题根本不是他的错，也许是上帝在惩罚他。

哥伦布让自己的两个弟弟巴尔托洛梅奥和迭戈负责指挥伊莎贝拉地区。这天是 1496 年 3 月 10 日，哥伦布将物资装满两只小船，起锚，启程返回西班牙。

第八章

第三次尝试

返程航行充满艰难险阻。他们在途中遭遇了强风和大浪。这次航行花了四个月，比预计的时间要长。补给品出现了短缺。当 1496 年 7 月哥伦布抵达加的斯时，他和他的船员看上去好像经历了一场仗。他们饥肠辘辘，疲惫不堪，衣服也像破布一样挂在身上。

哥伦布在斐迪南国王和伊莎贝拉女王面前为自己辩护。他告诉他们他已经带回了一些财宝。（这是事实。）他还说他探索了七百个岛屿。（这个说法夸张了！）

国王和女王很不高兴。哥伦布失败了。他没有把他承诺的东西带回来。王宫里的人称他为“蚊子上将”。哥伦布的儿子迭戈和斐迪南也在王宫。他们做了国王和女王的侍从。他们只能看着他们的父亲蒙受羞辱。

然而，两年后，国王和女王同意派遣哥伦布再次远航。他们为什么要这么做？

一个葡萄牙探险家瓦斯科·达·伽马已经真的到达了印度群岛。他沿非洲西海岸航行，绕过非洲大陆南端，抵达了印度。他带回了许多财宝。西班牙统治者不希望葡萄牙得到所有的财富。于是他们决定再试一次。也许哥伦布最终会在这次向西的航海中，找到财富，大赚一笔……

1498 年 5 月 30 日，四十六岁的哥伦布从西班牙南部开启了他的第三次远洋航行。他只有六只船。当然，这次的船队比第一次航行时规模更大。但是同样，他的船员再次由许多犯人组成。为什么？因为人们听说哥伦布失败了，没有人愿意跟着他航海了。

克里斯托弗·哥伦布

这些船朝西南方向的加那

利群岛驶去。在加纳利群岛，他们分成两支船队。三只船前往伊斯帕尼奥拉岛运送补给物资，另外三只船由哥伦布指挥，出发去探险。哥伦布再次遇到了麻烦。海面上没有风，因此他们只得漂浮前行。太阳非常炎热，船员们的皮肤晒起了水泡。他们的食物开始腐坏变质，他们的水桶在炽热的高温下也爆裂开来。这样的高温天气持续了八天。

后来，起风了，他们发现了土地。当时哥伦布一定欣喜万分。他用“三位一体”的含义给这个岛命名为“特立尼达拉”岛。

这个岛的另一侧就是哥伦布的最大发现——南美洲西海岸线。这片陆地看起来像一块大陆。但这怎么可能呢？哥伦布仍然相信自己已经找到了印度群岛。他断定

瓦斯科·达·伽马

瓦斯科·达·伽马

当瓦斯科·达·伽马决定绕非洲航行抵达印度群岛时，许多人以为他疯了。他们不认为大西洋与印度洋相连。（巴塞洛缪·迪亚士曾经航行到非洲南端，但没有从那里绕过去。）1497 年 7 月 8 日，瓦斯科·达·伽马从里斯本启航出发，证明了两大洋确实相连。1497 年 11 月 22 日，他带领他的船队绕过了非洲好望角。在非洲停留之后，1498 年 5 月 20 日，瓦斯科·达·伽马到达印度科泽科德。他和印度人进行商品贸易。在返航途中，他的许多船员死于坏血病，这是一种由缺乏维生素 C 引起的疾病。尽管如此，一到葡萄牙，瓦斯科·达·伽马就被当成英雄，受到人们的热烈欢迎。

他现在看到的一定是“人间天堂”或者是伊甸园。但是，他没有时间去探索这个天堂。他想返回伊斯帕尼奥拉岛。

哥伦布抵达圣多明各（他的弟弟们建立的新殖民地）后，迎接他的又是一件出人意料的糟糕事。这里不再由巴尔托洛梅奥和迭戈指挥了。这里没有食物，人们生了病，有人造起了反。哥伦布试图维持秩序，但他的运气并不比他的弟弟们好。

这年 8 月，国王和女王派人来查看到底发生了什么事。那人回去报告了。传言是真的。这里的情况一团糟。许多人生病了。另外的人——那些造反者——不是死了就是被关进了监狱。哥伦布和他的弟弟们被逮捕了，他们的手腕和脚踝上被戴上镣铐，他们被关进了监狱。

大西洋上将克里斯托弗·哥伦布戴着镣铐被送回了西班牙。

阿梅里戈·韦斯普奇

阿梅里戈·韦斯普奇是个探险家，南美洲和北美洲就是以他的名字命名的。1454年，他出生于意大利的佛罗伦萨，后来移居到西班牙的塞维利亚。韦斯普奇听说哥伦布航海的事迹后，非常渴望找到一条通往印度群岛的西部通道。他学会了航海和导航，多次前往委内瑞拉和巴西等地。尽管哥伦布认为这些地方是亚洲，但韦斯普奇准确地判断出这些地方不是亚洲。韦斯普奇意识到这些地方是一块新大陆的一部分。他让人画出了新地图。一个德国地图制作师建议把这个新大陆命名为美洲。

第九章

最后一次尝试

在西班牙，哥伦布被关进了监狱。他在监狱里待了六个礼拜。当镣铐被取下时，他把它们收藏了起来。他跟他的一个儿子说，他希望把这些镣铐和自己葬在一起。

大多数人不会有勇气请求国王和女王出钱再赞助一次航海。但克里斯托弗·哥伦布不是大多数人。他拒绝放弃。

国王和女王知道瓦斯科·达·伽马开始了另一次航海，他可能会带着各种珍奇异宝回来。为什么葡萄牙能得到所有的荣耀？于是，当哥伦布去拜见斐迪南和伊莎贝拉，请求派遣他第四次航海的时候，不管你信不信，他们居然同意了。但是这一次，他们只提供了四只老旧的船和一百三十五个人手，其中包括哥伦布十三岁的儿子斐迪南。这次还有规定：不许抓奴隶，不许在伊斯帕尼奥拉岛停留。

哥伦布并不在意这些规定，他唯一关心的是他能再次航海了。

1502 年 5 月 9 日，哥伦布和他的四只摇摇晃晃的船启程出发了。起初，万事顺利。白天，天气晴朗，阳光明媚。夜晚，星光闪烁，熠熠生辉。一阵和缓的风推动

船只平稳前行。但是后来，乌云翻滚，狂风大作。哥伦布闻到了湿重空气的味道。

一场飓风即将来临！

目前唯一明智的办法就是登陆最近的岛屿寻求庇护。最近的岛屿是伊斯帕尼奥拉岛。但是哥伦布被禁止踏足这个岛屿。新总督拒绝让他登陆。哥伦布非常气愤。这里是他建立定居点的地方！然而，他和他的船员却被迫待在船上，等待风暴过去。

哥伦布再次起航前往牙买加，但却遭遇了更多风暴。其中一次持续了八十八天。最终，哥伦布的船队“一瘸一拐”地登上了陆地——现在的尼加拉瓜——他们在这里停下来修补船只。

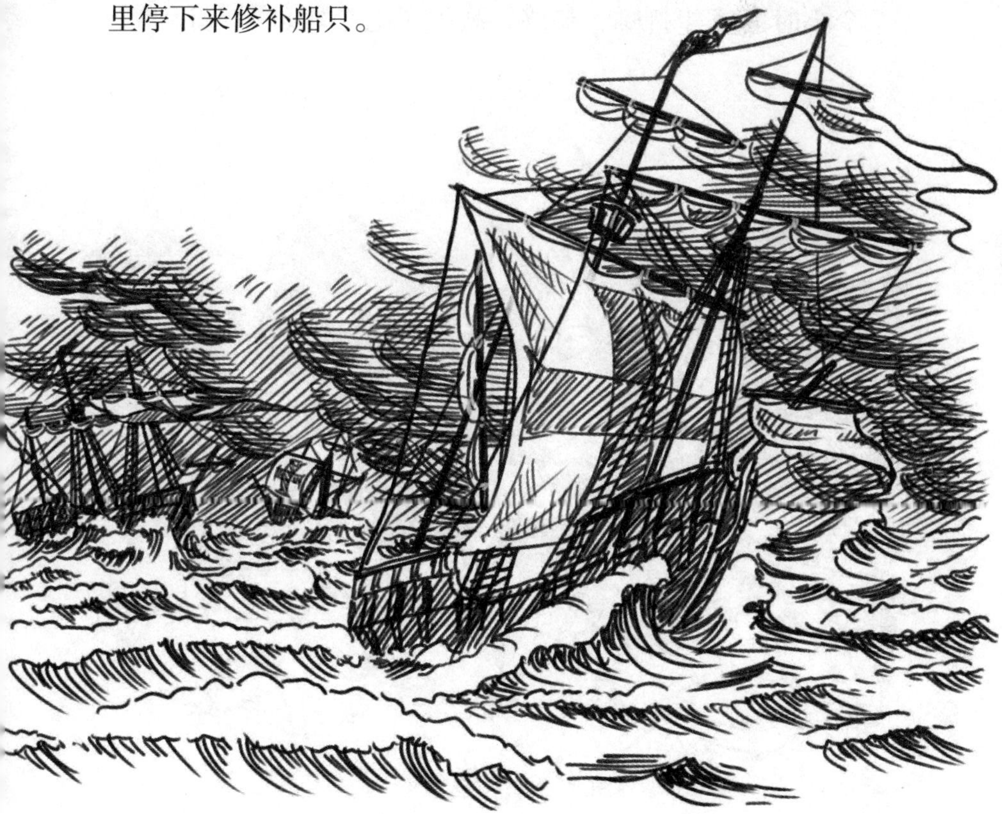

后来，在现在被称为巴拿马的北部，哥伦布终于发现了黄金！哥伦布开始建立另一个定居点。起初，当地的土著很友好。他们进行贸易，两个群体和平共处。但是好景不长。

到了春天，四百名土著带着弓箭来了。一场持续三个小时的战斗打响，最终，死掉了七个西班牙人和十个土著。

当时，哥伦布正生病，发着高烧。他独自一人留在一只船上。听到战斗打响，他爬上桅杆，爬到船只最高处，大声呼喊。但没有人回答他。他疲惫不堪，连连哭泣。不一会儿，他听到有个声音在告诉他不要害怕，一切都会没事的。

哥伦布振作精神，召集船员，放弃了这个定居点。他带着几只船离开了。这几只船破败不堪，都几乎要散架了。他们在牙买加海岸附近抛锚，并在那里停留了一年。

哥伦布和他的船员被困住了。但至少当地的土著看上去很友好。每天，他们给哥伦布和他的船员送来食物和水。但哥伦布并不信任他们。如果土

著不再提供食物怎么办？或者更糟糕的是，如果他们发动攻击怎么办？这一次，可再也没有能载着他们逃跑的船了。

哥伦布说服了两名船员迭戈·门德斯和巴尔托洛梅奥·菲耶斯基，让他们划独木舟前往伊斯帕尼奥拉岛。

他们可以在那里买一只船回来营救他们。起初，门德斯认为这个计划不可行。但他还是愿意冒险一试。哥伦布亲吻门德斯的双颊，祝福他和菲耶斯基一路平安。

迭戈·门德斯和巴尔托洛梅奥·菲耶斯基离开几天后，哥伦布对土著的担忧得到了证实。他们拒绝再提供任何补给物品。于是，哥伦布决定骗这些土著，让他们帮他做事情。哥伦布知道马上就会有月食。他告诉土著上帝对他们非常生气，停止供应食物和水是不对的。事实上上帝非常生气，因此他打算把月亮藏起来。这天晚上，当月食出现时，月亮确实“藏了起来”。土著被吓到了。他们答应继续送来食物，直到救援船到来的那一天。

1504 年 6 月 29 日，一只非常老旧的船驶向牙买加海岸。克里斯托弗·哥伦布快五十二岁了。现在他视力衰退，健康不佳，身体经常疼痛。尽管如此，他还是很高兴自己得救了。而且，他急着回去见女王。

但是他再也没有见到女王。他抵达西班牙的三个礼拜之后，女王去世了。那天是 1504 年 11 月 26 日，哥伦布失去了他最大的支持者。

哥伦布已经老迈，疾病缠身。他当探险记家的日子一去不复返了。1506 年 5 月 20 日，克里斯托弗·哥伦布与世长辞。直到去世时，他还认为自己找到了通往印度群岛的航海路线，但是他没有。

如果说他没有到达印度群岛，那他为什么这么出名呢？因为哥伦布发现了新土地——加勒比群岛、牙买加和古巴——这些以前其他欧洲人从未到过的地方。因为

有了哥伦布，欧洲和美洲之间才有了一条航海通道，其他探险家才可以沿着这条通道航行。

克里斯托弗·哥伦布没有找到黄金，但他却找到了一个全新的世界。

克里斯托弗·哥伦布生平年表

1451 年 — 克里斯托弗·哥伦布出生于意大利热那亚。
1477 年 — 哥伦布和弟弟在里斯本开了一家地图制作店。
1479 年 — 哥伦布娶贵族女子费莉帕·佩雷斯特雷洛·莫尼斯。
1490 年 — 儿子迭戈出生。
1484 年 — 哥伦布未能获取葡萄牙国王若奥二世的赞助。
1485 年 — 费莉帕去世，哥伦布前往西班牙。
1486 年 — 哥伦布的赞助请求被西班牙斐迪南国王和伊莎贝拉女王拒绝。
1491 年 — 哥伦布向斐迪南和伊莎贝拉再次请求赞助，但再次被拒绝。
1492 年 — 斐迪南国王和伊莎贝拉女王同意赞助哥伦布航海。8 月 3 日，“尼娜”号、“平塔”号和“圣玛丽亚”号向西启航，10 月 12 日，哥伦布登陆新大陆。
1493 年 — 3 月 15 日，哥伦布返回西班牙。9 月 25 日，哥伦布开启到新大陆的第二次航海。
1498 年 — 哥伦布开启从西班牙到新大陆的第三次航海。
1500 年 — 哥伦布被捕，戴着镣铐被送回西班牙。
1502 年 — 克里斯托弗·哥伦布最后的第四次航海。
1506 年 — 5 月 20 日，克里斯托弗·哥伦布于西班牙去世。

世界大事记

1271 年 — 马可·波罗经陆路从欧洲来中国旅行。
1401 年 — 佛罗伦萨举办圣乔凡尼洗礼堂青铜大门的设计竞赛。
1420 年 — 扬·凡·艾克完善油画技法。
1431 年 — 圣女贞德被绑在火刑柱上烧死。
1433 年 — 中国终止所有远洋航行，切断国外往来。
1438 年 — 南美的印加帝国成为世界上最大的帝国。
1439 年 — 约翰内斯·古腾堡发明印刷机。
1453 年 — 君士坦丁堡（今伊斯坦布尔）落入奥斯曼土耳其人手中。
1487 年 — 巴塞洛缪·迪亚士绕非洲南端航行。
1492 年 — 斐迪南和伊莎贝拉将所有犹太人驱离西班牙。
1497 年 — 瓦斯科·达·伽马航行到印度。
1503 年 — 莱奥纳尔多·达·芬奇画《蒙娜丽莎》。
1506 年 — 罗马圣彼得大教堂开始建造。
1508 年 — 米开朗琪罗开始画西斯廷教堂天顶壁画。

Who Was Christopher Columbus?

A tall man paced the deck of his ship. He and his men had been at sea for seventy days, since August 3, 1492. They had sailed over 2,650 miles from Spain. Now, land had been spotted. Had Christopher Columbus's dream to reach the Indies finally come true?

For years he had begged the rulers of Portugal and Spain to give him money for this journey. He wanted to find a route from Europe to the Indies by sailing west. The Indies included China, Japan, and India. No one had done this before.

As the sun rose on October 12, 1492, Columbus and his crew made their way to shore.

Falling to his knees, he kissed the ground and cried. Oh, what riches awaited him! He would return to Spain a hero.

Columbus didn't know that this was not the Indies. So where was he? Columbus and his crew were on land that no one in Europe knew about. Christopher Columbus had discovered a new world.

Chapter 1

An Explorer Is Born

In 1451, a boy named Cristoforo Colombo was born in the city of Genoa, Italy. In the English-speaking world, he is known as Christopher Columbus.

Christopher's father was a wool weaver. His mother was the daughter of a weaver, and she helped with the work. It was expected that one day Christopher would take over the family business.

But young Christopher did not want to follow in his father's footsteps. He loved the sea, the smell of the salty air. He loved the way the wind blew through his hair. Genoa was a busy port on the Mediterranean Sea. Christopher and his younger brother, Bartolomeo, loved going down to the docks. They watched ships come into port, bringing in goods such as silk, tea, and spices from the East. And they watched the ships leave, loaded with wool, copper, tin, and weapons. Christopher hoped to work on one of those ships one day.

At that time, boys as young as ten went off to sea as cabin boys. A cabin boy did all sorts of jobs—cooking, cleaning, fetching tools and supplies. Christopher got his first job aboard a ship when he was about fourteen.

Christopher split his time between helping his father and sailing the seas. He sailed to such places as Ireland and Iceland. He learned a lot about how to steer a ship in the open sea. This skill would be very important later in his life.

At nineteen, Christopher had grown into a strong young man. No one knows exactly what he looked like. Some say he was tall with wide shoulders. His skin was said to be pale, and he is believed to have had red hair and light blue eyes. Not only was his body strong, but his mind was sharp. Some said he was too stubborn and had a bad temper. He was also very, very sure of himself. Once he set his mind on something, he never let it go. And Christopher Columbus was very sure about one thing—he wanted to become a famous sea captain. Famous and rich.

Chapter 2

Mapping the World

In 1476, when Christopher was twenty-five years old, he was on a ship attacked by French warships. The ship went up in flames. But Christopher managed to reach the shore.

He was near a small fishing village in Portugal. Some villagers found him and took care of him. Christopher was happy for their help. However, he did not want to stay in a quiet village. He soon made his way to the capital city of Lisbon.

For nine years he lived in Lisbon. His brother Bartolomeo lived there, too, and they opened a business together. They were mapmakers. This was a perfect job for a man who wanted to learn more about the world. At the docks, the brothers would meet the captains of incoming ships. They would collect information and create maps based on what the captains told them.

At the map store, Christopher heard merchants talking about trying to find a new route from Europe to eastern lands known as the Indies. Why were these merchants so interested in traveling there? Spices. Spices such as pepper, ginger, cloves, and cinnamon. People used spices in cooking to flavor food. In Egypt, Italian merchants could buy spices from the Indies. Then they sold them all over Europe for a lot of money. But if an explorer found a route directly to the Indies, he could buy up spices. There would be no need to rely on the Italian merchants. Whoever found a sea route to the Indies would grow rich from the spice trade.

At that time, most people knew the world was round. What they didn't know was how big it was. It was thought that one landmass— Europe and Asia and Africa— was surrounded by one body of water called the Ocean Sea.

The only travelers so far to reach the Indies had gone by land. *The Description of the World*, written by the explorer Marco Polo, told of his travels from Italy to China. Columbus read the book. He was fascinated by Marco Polo's stories of rubies as big as a man's fist, and palaces with floors made of gold.

Columbus was determined to be the first to *sail* all the way to the Indies. The king of Portugal had tried to send ships to the Indies by following a route around Africa, then east. But the ships kept turning back. The sailors said this route was too long. And they did not know where they were going. But Columbus had another idea. A *better* idea, he thought. He would sail *west* to the Indies.

He would sail straight across the Ocean Sea!

Other people laughed at his plan. Sail across the Ocean Sea? Why, that would take months! Columbus wouldn't be able take along enough food and water. How would he and the crew survive?

Marco Polo and the Silk Road

In 1271, Marco Polo accompanied his father and uncle to the East, arriving in Shangdu in 1275 to meet the ruler, Kublai Khan. Over the next two hundred years, trade between India, China, and Europe grew. Merchants traveled the overland route, known as the Silk Road, and traded goods such as silk, pearls, gold, rubies, pepper, nutmeg, cloves, and tea. But the road was long and dangerous. Travelers had to cross deserts and mountains. Bandits waited to rob them of their goods. By the fifteenth century, Europeans desperately wanted to find another way to the Indies.

Christopher had no answer for these questions. So he read more. He read book after book about traveling the world. One book said there were only three thousand nautical miles between the Canary Islands and Japan. Japan was a place in the Indies where Columbus wanted to go!

Another book about the Indies claimed there were men with umbrella-shaped feet, people with eyes on their shoulders, and creatures that were half lion and half eagle! Most people thought these stories were made up. Still, the more Columbus read, the more excited he became.

Even more important to Christopher Columbus was his belief that God meant for him to make the journey to the Indies. He believed God had given him the love of the sea. God had brought him to Portugal. And God would guide him in his travels.

Chapter 3

Waiting and More Waiting

What Christopher needed was someone to give him the money for his trip. Someone who was rich. And powerful. Someone like the king of Portugal. But how would Christopher meet the king? He needed an in, a connection.

In 1478, Christopher Columbus married Felipa Perestrello e Moniz. Her family had friends at the king's court.

But it wasn't until 1484 that Christopher Columbus finally met King John II of Portugal. Columbus stood tall in front of the king. He told him he knew the right way to get to the Indies. He was sure of it. And Columbus promised to bring back lots and lots of gold. King John listened to this big talker. And what did the king say? He said no.

Christopher Columbus was not discouraged. If the king of Portugal wouldn't support him, maybe King Ferdinand and Queen Isabella of Spain would.

While Christopher was waiting to meet King John, his wife had died. So when Christopher went to Spain, he left their young son, Diego, in the care of monks at a monastery. A young boy would not survive a dangerous journey across the sea.

Columbus had to wait nine months to see Queen Isabella and King Ferdinand. Why? In those days, the Spanish royal court moved from city to city. Columbus could not afford to follow the court, so he settled in the city of Córdoba to wait. There he met a young peasant girl named Beatriz Enríquez de Harana. Two years later, Beatriz gave birth to Columbus's second son, a boy named Ferdinand.

Then, finally, on May 1, 1486, Columbus got to meet King Ferdinand and Queen Isabella. He was hopeful that the king and queen would say yes to the voyage. They would see what a good Christian Columbus was. He would spread the faith throughout the new lands. Plus, his trip would help make Spain very rich.

But Spain was in the middle of a costly war. There was no money now for a long trip to the Indies. Columbus would have to wait. More waiting? Oh no!

Two years went by. Columbus tried asking King John II of Portugal for money again. But he was too busy—busy celebrating the return of another explorer, Bartholomew Diaz. Columbus's plan to sail west still seemed foolish to King John.

So it was back to Spain for Columbus. The war Ferdinand and Isabella were fighting went on for three more years. All that time, Columbus waited. And when he went back to see the king and queen, at last he got the answer he was waiting for.

Yes!

Columbus was now forty-one years old. That was old to be setting out on such a hard journey.

He was angry about the long years of waiting. So he made some demands.

Bartholomew Diaz

Anxious to find a trade route to India, King John II of Portugal sent Bartholomew Diaz on a voyage. Diaz left Lisbon in August 1487. Despite terrible weather, he and his crew realized that it was possible to sail around the southern tip of Africa. They called it the Cape of Storms, because of the terrible weather they encountered there. (It was later renamed the Cape of Good Hope.) Diaz returned to Portugal in 1488, a hero. Although he didn't sail all the way around the tip of Africa—Vasco da Gama did that in 1497—Diaz was credited with helping to open up a new trade route with the East.

What did he want? Well, if he was successful, he wanted the title of Admiral of the Ocean Sea. He wanted to rule all the lands he discovered. And he wanted to be able to keep one-tenth of any treasure he found there.

Queen Isabella did not believe what she was hearing. Who was this arrogant man? She would not give in to his demands. No, Queen Isabella was through with Christopher Columbus!

So what did Christopher Columbus do? He packed his bags, saddled up his mule, and went to see the king of France. Maybe he would send Columbus on the voyage.

As Columbus started on his way, he heard hoofbeats behind him. It was Queen Isabella's men. She had changed her mind. She wasn't about to let the king of France get riches that could be hers. And if Columbus failed, well, then nothing would be lost; neither Isabella nor the French king would get a thing.A contract was signed.

Columbus's journey was about to begin.

Chapter 4

On the Ocean Sea

Now Christopher Columbus needed ships and a crew. Queen Isabella ordered the people from the town of Palos to give Columbus two ships. Palos had supported her enemies in the war, and she wanted to punish the town.

It was expensive to make ships. But the townspeople had to obey her.

The two ships from Palos were called the *Niña* and the *Pinta*. They were caravels—small but fast. But Columbus also wanted something bigger. He looked and looked. The biggest ship he could find, the sixty-foot-long *Santa María*, was a slow cargo boat. Still he decided to make do.

Two brothers from Palos, Martín and Vicente Pinzón,

The Nao and the Caravel

The nao (pronounce it like this: now) and the caravel were two types of ships that could sail long distances. The nao was a big, heavy, slow ship with three or four masts. It was good for carrying cargo. It was also stable on rough seas. And it had a lot of room, so a lot of food and water could be stored for long voyages. The caravel was a newer type of ship. It had one to three masts and was lighter than the nao.

signed on to serve as captains. Martín would command the *Pinta*, Vicente the *Niña*. Columbus would be the captain of the *Santa María*. He was also in charge of the entire fleet.

As for the crew, it was hard to find men willing to go. Most people thought Columbus's idea to sail west was crazy.

After begging, pleading, and even threatening, Columbus got about ninety men to join his crew. Many were friends or relatives of the Pinzón brothers. Others were criminals. They were freed from jail to sail with Columbus. Twenty-four men were to sail on the *Niña*, twenty-six on the *Pinta*, and forty on the *Santa María*.

Most of the men were sailors. But there were also men to repair the ships, men to fish, men to clean, and men to make barrels. Columbus also took along a secretary and a doctor. No women were on board. (In those days, no women were sailors.)

The ships were loaded with supplies. Ropes and maps and compasses. Fresh and dried meat, milk, fruit, eggs, sardines, anchovies, olive oil, raisins, biscuits, cheese, peas, garlic, onions, rice, and beans. And many barrels of water. They took cannons, crossbows, and muskets in case of run-ins with enemy ships. And for trading, they took bells, scissors, knives, coins, beads, and mirrors.

If Columbus expected a farewell party, he was wrong. The people of Palos were angry about paying for Columbus's ships. Instead of cheering, they booed.

It was August 2, 1492. Christopher Columbus gathered his men onshore to pray. They prayed for a safe journey. They prayed that they would find new lands and riches.

Then, in the early hours of August 3, 1492, the *Niña*, the *Pinta*, and the *Santa María* set sail from Palos. Columbus's plan was to sail south to the Canary Islands. From there, he would turn west, toward Cipangu (known today as Japan). Columbus thought that the path from the Canary Islands to Cipangu would follow a straight line. He thought that he just had to sail 2,400 miles west from the Canaries to reach the

Indies. That was his plan, but it was wrong.

The three ships dropped their anchors at the Canary Islands. Columbus and Martín Pinzón went ashore and bought more goods—glass beads, brass bells, brightly dyed cloth, jewelry, and mirrors. These could be traded in the Indies. They also loaded the ships with fresh food.

On September 6, 1492, they set sail once again. Columbus led the way in the *Santa María*. The first few days on the open sea were smooth sailing. The men seemed happy. They sang songs and fished off the sides of the ships. And when the sun set, the men gathered together and prayed.

The crew slept in two shifts. One crew worked during the day. The other crew worked at night.

But as the days went by, the crew grew restless. They had been at sea a long time. Just how far had they come? Well, Columbus kept two logbooks. In one, he recorded the real distance sailed each day. In the other— the one that his crew could look at—he recorded fewer miles. According to

Columbus, he didn't want to scare the crew by letting them think the voyage was taking too long.

But the men were scared, anyway. They were out in the middle of the ocean. What would they find? Would they ever return home? So Columbus kept talking about all the riches that awaited them.

The men were on the lookout for any sign of land. Anything gave them hope. A bit of seaweed on the water. Birds flying together.

On September 25, Martín Pinzón thought he saw land. But no, he hadn't.

For more than two weeks more, the ships sailed on. Most of the men had never been on a trip that lasted so long. To them, those weeks seemed like forever!

And life on the ship was not pleasant. Columbus's crew did not bathe or brush their teeth. They walked the deck in their bare feet. Sometimes, they stepped on a bug or a rat dropping. And what happened when they needed to go to the bathroom? They went over the side of the ship!

On each ship, the only cabin was for the captain. The rest of the crew slept wherever they could find a dry spot—on top of a coil of rope or next to a barrel.

There were no cooks. The men had to prepare food themselves. But first they had to battle the mice and rats that tried to get the food! Sometimes, fish were caught and salted and dried. If the crew wanted to make biscuits, they would first have to pick insects out of the flour. Most of the time, the food was rotten or didn't taste good. So they put a lot of garlic in it to hide the bad taste. And they usually ate at night so they wouldn't have to see what was crawling around in their food!

The ships were very dirty. Rats scurried over the wooden planks. Fleas were everywhere. And there were lice. Everyone got lice!

The mood aboard the ships got worse each day. Some of the men thought Columbus was going crazy. They had seen him pacing the deck, staring at the sky. Where was this madman taking them? Some men wanted to toss Columbus overboard. Then they could head home.

On October 7, there was another false sighting of land. Columbus now promised that if land wasn't reached in three days, he would turn the fleet around.

Luckily, on the night of October 10, Columbus thought he saw land.

This time it was true. Just after midnight on October 12, a crewmember from the *Pinta* shouted, "*Tierra! Tierra*!" (Land! Land!)

Yes, the faint outline of land could be seen. Everyone rejoiced. They had reached the Indies. Or so they thought.

Chapter 5

Land Ho!

As soon as the sun rose on October 12, Columbus was ready to go ashore. He and his officers put on their best clothes and piled into small rowboats. They had a Spanish flag and items to trade. They also took swords and knives, in case they met unfriendly natives.

What riches were they about to find? Gold? Spices?

Columbus stepped onto the strange land, fell to his knees, and kissed the ground. He thanked God for leading him here. Columbus planted the flag and claimed the land for Spain. He named it San Salvador.

Watching Columbus from behind bushes were some of the island's native inhabitants. They were called the Taino.

Slowly, they crept closer. Columbus and his men stared at these strange people. They were not wearing gold and silk. In fact, they were hardly wearing anything at all!

The natives were equally surprised. The Taino had never seen white men or people wearing clothes or people with beards. And the ships out in the sea? How strange they were!

Columbus thought this island was off the coast of the Indies. So he called the people he met "Indians." Of course, the island was nowhere near the Indies. Columbus's ships had actually landed in what is today known as the Bahamas. The island of San Salvador was beautiful. Lush trees, winding rivers, a big sparkling lake.

The Taino gave the Spaniards cotton, wooden spears, and parrots. Lots and lots of colorful and noisy parrots! In return, the Taino got glass beads and bells.

But where were the palaces with gold floors? Where were all the riches and spices? Columbus saw that some Taino had small gold rings in their noses. There must be gold

The Taino

The Taino people were ruled by a chief. It could be a man or a woman. Families lived in buildings made from wooden poles, woven straw, and leaves. The Taino were excellent farmers, fishermen, and hunters. They were also skilled wood-carvers, and they wove beautiful hammocks out of cotton. They worshipped many different gods. Columbus believed his mission was to convert them all to Christianity. The Taino lived happily and peacefully before columbus arrived. europeans brought diseases such as smallpox, measles, and the flu. In thirty years, between 80 and 90 percent of the Taino died.

Why Gold?

Gold has always been valuable because it is so rare and beautiful. Between the years 1370 and 1420, many big gold mines in Europe ran out of gold. So European merchants began traveling to Africa and Asia in search of gold. The race to find gold was fierce. Later, in 1511 (after Columbus's death), King Ferdinand proclaimed, " Get gold, humanely if you can, but at all hazards, get gold!" In a short time, the Inca and Aztec civilizations in Central America, which were rich with gold, were destroyed by Spanish conquerors.

somewhere, Columbus reasoned.

Columbus tried using signs and gestures to communicate. He waved his arms and asked where the gold was. Through signs, the natives told him there was an island to the south that had gold. That must be China, Columbus thought.

On October 14, Columbus and his crew set off. But before they pulled up their anchors, they kidnapped several Taino and took them on board. These men would be taught Spanish and could serve as interpreters on the other islands.

The *Niña*, *Pinta*, and *Santa María* spent two weeks sailing around different islands. They met many friendly natives. They were given a lot of cotton and spears and parrots. But no gold.

Columbus turned to the Indians for help. They signed for him to sail south to another island. Columbus thought they were talking about Japan. On October 28, the *Niña*, the *Pinta*, and the *Santa María* arrived at this next island. When Columbus saw natives wearing gold around their wrists and ankles, he became excited. This wasn't Japan, Columbus decided. It was China! Even better!

Once again, Columbus was wrong. He was actually in Cuba. Columbus sent a group of men to introduce themselves to the famous ruler of China, the Great Khan. But of course the group came back with no sign of the Great Khan. Worse yet, there was no gold here. It was time to move on.

Chapter 6

Shipwreck!

By early December, the *Pinta* had gone off on its own to find gold. The weather was turning colder and stormy. If the *Niña* and the *Santa María* were to return to Spain before winter set in, they had to leave soon.

But there was still more to explore, Columbus thought, so he ordered his ships to sail. On December 6, Columbus named the island they landed on Hispaniola, because the trees there reminded him of Spain.

Then on Christmas Eve, disaster struck. Some men were celebrating. After a long night, Columbus went to sleep. So did most of the crew of the *Santa María*. One of the ship's boys was left in charge.

The wind was calm. And the ship was moving at a slow pace. Yet, sometime after midnight, the *Santa María* crashed into a coral reef. A cry rang out and Columbus was awoken. Desperately, he tried to save the ship. But it was too late. Her sides had ripped open.

The *Santa María* was sinking!

Columbus called for help. A local Taino chief sent men in canoes. They unloaded the *Santa María*, and brought the goods and supplies ashore.

Besides helping unload the ship, the natives brought gold! Not a lot, just a few samples— masks, jewelry, and other small trinkets.

After he got over the shock of losing a ship, Columbus took the sinking of the *Santa María* as a sign. God meant for him to go ashore on this island. After all, the chief had given Columbus rings, necklaces, and masks made of gold. And gold was what he had come for! Perhaps now they could go home.

But Columbus only had one ship left. Martín Pinzón and the *Pinta* were still missing. They couldn't all return to Spain on the small *Niña*. So Columbus built a fort. Forty men would remain there through the winter. They would look for gold. When Columbus returned, he would bring them (and the gold) home.

Columbus used wood from the *Santa María* to build the fort. A moat was dug around the fort, and the *Santa María's* cannons were put up. Columbus named the fort La Navidad. That is Spanish for "Christmas."

The *Niña* was loaded with fresh food and water. With what little gold he had, Columbus headed home on January 4, 1493.

After two days at sea, the *Niña* came upon an amazing sight. The *Pinta*! The two ships met and continued the voyage home together until a bad storm separated them again.

Columbus feared that the *Pinta* might be lost forever. The storm grew fiercer. What if they drowned? Then nobody would know that the voyage had been successful. So Columbus grabbed a piece of parchment and wrote about his discovery of new lands. He wrapped the letter in cloth, covered it in a cake of wax, and placed it in a barrel. Hopefully, one day, someone would find the barrel and read about what Columbus had accomplished.

The storm raged for fifteen days. Even so, Columbus sailed on. After all, what choice did he have?

On March 15, Columbus dropped anchor in the waters of Palos. It had been almost seven and a half months since he had last seen this beautiful harbor. What joy he must have felt. And, amazingly, the *Pinta* had also made it home safely.

Of course, King Ferdinand and Queen Isabella wanted to see Columbus right away. So he set off for Barcelona. Everywhere, people ran out into the streets to catch a glimpse of Columbus and his crew. The people had never seen Indians or parrots or corn before.

At last, Columbus reached the royal court. There, under

a golden canopy, sat Ferdinand and Isabella. As Columbus approached the king and queen, the royal couple stood up! Only a great lord would receive such a greeting. Columbus kissed their hands and sat down next to them. Then he described his journey. Columbus showed off the treasures he had brought back. Colorful parrots. Gold nose rings. Not a lot of gold, to be sure. But some. And he had brought corn. Yams. Yucca. No one was laughing at Christopher Columbus now.

Best of all, the king and queen kept their word. Columbus was given the title Admiral of the Ocean Sea. He was made governor-general of all the lands he discovered. And he got to keep one-tenth of all the treasure he had brought back.

Christopher Columbus was a hero. He rode through Barcelona seated next to the king. People cheered. This was the greatest moment of his life.

Soon, his glory days would be over.

Chapter 7

On the Sea Again

Orders were given for Columbus's second trip. He was to return to Hispaniola, bring back the crew left there, and leave more men to settle the land.

Columbus was elated. Here was another chance to bring back gold.

On his first voyage, Columbus practically had to beg men to join him. This time, between 1,200 and 1,500 men eagerly volunteered. Who knew what riches would be found on the trip?

Now the crew included priests (to convert the natives), noblemen, farmers, and other skilled laborers. Even Columbus's younger brother Diego signed on.

Columbus was given seventeen ships. The *Niña* was part of the fleet. Columbus commanded a ship called the *Santa María* in honor of the one that had been wrecked.

The ships were loaded with food and water. This time horses were brought along for the men to use once they reached land, as well as sheep and pigs to live on farms, and seeds of wheat and barley to plant.

On September 25, 1493, the ships set off from the port of Cadiz. This time, it was a much easier trip across the ocean. Columbus knew the way. No one complained.

Columbus checked out new islands. He found cotton, more colorful parrots, and fruit. And, oh, the scenery! Green mountains. Wide valleys. Sparkling rivers. Foamy white waterfalls. But they also saw awful things. Women were captured and made slaves. Humans ate other humans. (They are called cannibals.) Columbus and his crew didn't stay very long on those islands!

On the night of November 27, 1493, the ships arrived

The Islands of Columbus's Second Voyage

On his way back to Hispaniola, Columbus and his crew stopped at many islands. Dominica was the first island they came to. Columbus named it Dominica because it was discovered on a Sunday (November 3, 1493). On GuadEloupe, Columbus and his men tasted pineapple for the first time. Santa Maria la Redonda was the "round island." He also discovered the Virgin Islands and Puerto Rico.

in Hispaniola. Right away, one of the ships fired a cannon. There was no response from the shore. Where were the men who had stayed behind? What could have happened to them? Columbus and his crew were scared.

Suddenly, they heard the sound of oars slapping the water. Could it be Columbus's men? No. It was a canoe filled with Taino. And they were bringing terrible news. The fort had burned down. All the Spaniards were dead. What had happened? It was unclear. Some said the Spaniards fought among themselves and killed each other. Others said the settlers had gotten sick and died. Still others claimed a nearby tribe killed the Spaniards and burned down the settlement. Whatever the true story was, La Navidad was gone. A new settlement had to be built from scratch.

In a hot, swampy area with no clean water, Columbus and his crew began to build a new colony. They called it Isabella in honor of their queen. It was a bad spot to choose. Mosquitoes and gnats swarmed around the men, biting their flesh.

The men were not happy. This was not why they had come on the voyage. They wanted gold. To make matters worse, many men fell ill. Perhaps they got sick from the bug bites. Perhaps it was because there wasn't enough food to eat. The crops they planted weren't growing well. Or maybe they were just plain tired.

There was no choice but to send some of the fleet back to Spain for food and medicine. So on February 2, 1494, twelve ships returned home.

Columbus remained behind. Why? His desire to find gold made him stay. He sent many groups of healthy men to search for it. But each time, they came back empty-handed. They found specks of gold here and there in riverbeds. But not nearly enough to satisfy the king and queen.

Word reached Columbus of rich goldfields at a place called Cibao. So Columbus left his brother Diego in charge of Isabella and set off. Some gold was found, but just as before, not a lot.

Where was Cipangu, the island that Marco Polo had described? For the first time, Columbus was starting to grow nervous.

Columbus took three ships and sailed back to Cuba as well as to other islands he had visited. When Columbus returned to Hispaniola at the end of September 1494, he was very ill. And he still didn't have much gold.

Back at Isabella, the mosquitoes seemed to have gotten larger. His men were getting sicker. And angrier. Things were worse for the Taino, too. Columbus demanded that the Taino find gold for him. Every adult had to supply a certain amount of it or face severe punishment.

The Taino tried to fight back. However, their simple swords, bows, and arrows were no match for the Spaniards' weapons. They had crossbows and muskets.

With no gold for King Ferdinand and Queen Isabella, Columbus decided to take many Taino back to Spain as slaves. It was a terrible thing to do. But Columbus felt that it was his right. After all, he had claimed the land for Spain. So wasn't it his right to claim the people, too? The answer, of course, was no—it wasn't his right. Still, Columbus loaded ships with five hundred Taino and sent them off to Spain. Perhaps the slaves could be sold at market and bring in money.

Columbus was also nervous because he knew that word had gotten back to Ferdinand and Isabella that Columbus was not a good leader. He was stubborn. And arrogant.

Columbus concluded that he had to return to Spain to defend himself. Nothing that was going wrong was his fault. Perhaps God was punishing him.

Columbus put his brothers Bartolomeo and Diego in charge of Isabella. It was March 10, 1496. He loaded up two small ships. Raising the anchors, Columbus headed back to Spain.

Chapter 8

A Third Try

The return trip was rough. There were strong winds and high seas. The trip took four months, longer than expected. Supplies ran short. When Columbus reached Cadiz in July 1496, he and his men looked as though they had been through a war. They were hungry and tired. Their clothes hung on their bodies like rags.

Columbus defended himself before King Ferdinand and Queen Isabella. He told them he had brought back some treasure. (This was true.) And he said he had explored seven hundred islands. (This was an exaggeration!)

The king and queen were not happy. Columbus had failed. He had not brought back what he had promised.

Members of the court called him " Admiral of the Mosquitoes." Columbus's sons, Diego and Ferdinand, were there. They served as pages to the king and queen. They had to watch as their father was disgraced.

Yet, two years later, the king and queen agreed to send Columbus on another voyage. Why did they do this?

An explorer from Portugal, Vasco da Gama, had actually reached the Indies. He had sailed down the west coast of Africa, around the tip of the continent, and on to India. He brought back many riches. The rulers of Spain did not want Portugal getting all the treasure. So they decided to take another chance. Maybe Columbus, on this next voyage sailing west, would strike it rich . . . finally.

Forty-six-year-old Columbus began his third voyage from southern Spain on May 30, 1498. He had just six ships. Sure, it was a larger fleet than his first voyage. But once again, his crew was made up of many criminals. Why? Because people had heard of Columbus's failures. No one wanted to sail with him!

The ships sailed southwest to the Canary Islands. There they split into two groups. Three ships went to Hispaniola to deliver supplies. The other three, under Columbus' s command, went off exploring. Once again Columbus ran into trouble. There was no wind, so they just floated. The sun was hot, so the men's skin blistered. Their food began to rot, and their water barrels burst in the blazing heat. The heat lasted for eight days.

Then the winds picked up, and land was spotted. Columbus must have been overjoyed. He named this island Trinidad after the Holy Trinity.

Just across from this island lay what could have been Columbus' s biggest discovery— the coastline of South America. The land looked like a continent. But how could that be? Columbus was still sure that he had already found the Indies. Columbus reasoned that what he saw now must be the "Earthly Paradise," or the Garden of Eden. He had no

Vasco da Gama

When Vasco da Gama decided to try reaching the Indies by sailing around Africa, many people thought he was crazy. They did not think that the Atlantic Ocean connected with the Indian Ocean. (Bartholomew Diaz had sailed to the tip of Africa, but not around it.) On July 8, 1497, da Gama set sail from Lisbon and proved that the oceans did indeed connect. He guided his ships around Africa's Cape of Good Hope on November 22, 1497. After making stops in Africa, Vasco da Gama reached Calicut, India, on May 20, 1498. He traded goods with the people of India. On the return trip, many of his crewmembers died from scurvy, a disease caused by a lack of vitamin C. Nonetheless, upon arriving in Portugal, Vasco da Gama was greeted as a hero.

time to explore this paradise though; he wanted to get back to Hispaniola.

Arriving in Santo Domingo (a new colony his brothers had established), Columbus was greeted by another nasty surprise. Bartolomeo and Diego were no longer in command. There was no food. People were sick. Some had rebelled. Columbus tried to maintain order. He had no better luck than his brothers.

That August, the king and queen sent someone to see exactly what was going on. He reported back. The rumors were true. Things were a mess. Many men were sick. Others—ones who had rebelled—were dead or in jail. Columbus and his brothers were arrested. Shackles were slapped around their wrists and ankles. They were thrown in jail.

Christopher Columbus, Admiral of the Ocean Sea, was sent back to Spain in chains.

Amerigo Vespucci

Amerigo Vespucci is the explorer after whom North and South America are named. He was born in Florence, Italy, in 1454 and moved to Seville, Spain. Hearing about Columbus's voyages made Vespucci eager to find a western passage to the Indies. He learned to sail and navigate, making several trips to places such as Venezuela and Brazil. He rightly concluded that this was not Asia, despite what Columbus had thought. Vespucci realized that these places were part of a new continent. He had new maps drawn up. A German mapmaker suggested that this New World be called America.

Chapter 9

One Last Try

In Spain, Columbus landed in jail. There he stayed for six weeks. When his chains were taken off, he kept them. He told one of his sons that he wanted to be buried with them.

Most men wouldn't have had the nerve to ask the king and queen for more money for yet another voyage. But Christopher Columbus was not most men. He refused to give up.

The king and queen knew that Vasco da Gama was off on another voyage. He might come back with all sorts of treasure. Why should Portugal get all the glory? So, when Columbus went to Ferdinand and Isabella asking to be sent on a fourth voyage, believe it or not, they said yes. This time, though, they only provided four old ships and 135 men, including Columbus's thirteen year-old son, Ferdinand. And there were rules: No slaves. No stopping off at Hispaniola.

Columbus didn't mind about the rules: All he cared about was going to sea again.

On May 9, 1502, Columbus and his four rickety ships set off. At first, everything was perfect. The sky was clear. The sun was shining. The stars twinkled at night. And a steady wind moved the ships along. But then the clouds rolled in. The wind picked up. Columbus sniffed the heavy air.

A hurricane was on its way!

The only sensible thing to do was to seek shelter on the nearest island. That was Hispaniola. But Columbus had been forbidden to set foot there. The new governor refused to let him come ashore. Columbus was outraged. This was the place he had settled! Yet he and his men were forced to stay on their ships and wait out the storm.

Columbus next set sail for Jamaica, only to be hit by more storms. One lasted for eighty-eight days. At last, Columbus's ships limped to land— what is modern-day Nicaragua—where they stopped for repairs.

Then, finally, north of what is now Panama, Columbus found gold. At long last! He started another settlement. At first, the natives were friendly. They traded, and the two groups lived alongside each other in peace. But not for long.

In the spring, four hundred natives appeared carrying bows and arrows. A battle began that lasted for three hours. In the end, seven Spaniards and ten natives lay dead.

At the time, Columbus was sick with a high fever. So he was alone on one of the ships. Hearing the battle, he climbed up the mast to the highest point of the ship and cried out. There was no reply. Tired and sobbing, Columbus soon heard a voice telling him not to be afraid. Everything was going to be okay.

Gathering up his strength, Columbus collected his men

and abandoned the settlement. He left with a couple ships that were in such terrible shape, they were practically in pieces. They anchored off the coast of Jamaica. And that was where they stayed for the next year.

Columbus and his men were stranded. At least the natives seemed friendly. Each day, they brought Columbus and his men food to eat and water to drink. But Columbus did not trust them. What if the natives stopped bringing food? Or worse, what if they attacked? This time, there were no ships to escape on.

Columbus convinced two of his men, Diego Méndez and Bartolomeo Fieschi, to take a canoe and paddle to Hispaniola. There they could buy a ship and come back to rescue them. At first Méndez thought this was an impossible plan. But he took the risk, anyway. Columbus kissed Méndez on both his cheeks and bid him and Fieschi a safe journey.

A few days after Méndez and Fieschi left, Columbus's fears about the natives proved true. They refused to bring any more supplies. So Columbus decided to trick the natives into doing what he wanted. Knowing that there would soon be a lunar eclipse, Columbus told them God was very angry with them. It was wrong to stop bringing food and water. God was so angry, in fact, that he was going to hide the moon. When the eclipse appeared that night, and the moon did indeed "hide," the natives were scared. They promised to keep bringing food. And they did until the day the rescue ship arrived.

On June 29, 1504, a very old ship sailed to the coast of Jamaica. Christopher Columbus was almost fifty-two years old. Now his eyesight was failing. He was in poor health and in constant pain. Still, he was happy to be rescued. And he was anxious to get home to see the queen.

But he never set eyes on Queen Isabella again. Three weeks after his arrival in Spain, the queen died. It was November 26, 1504. Columbus had lost his biggest supporter.

Columbus was old and sick. His days as an explorer

were over. On May 20, 1506, Christopher Columbus died. He died believing that he had found a sea route to the Indies. But he had not.

So if he didn't reach the Indies, then why is he so famous? Columbus found new lands— Caribbean islands, Jamaica, and Cuba—places that no other European had ever been to. Because of Columbus, there was now a passageway between Europe and the Americas, one that other explorers could follow.

Christopher Columbus did not find gold; instead he found a whole new world.

Timeline of Christopher Columbus's Life

1451	Born in Genoa, Italy.
1477	Opens a mapmaking shop with his brother in Lisbon.
1479	Marries a noblewoman named Felipa Perestrello e Moniz.
1490	His son Diego is born.
1484	Fails to gain the patronage of King John II of Portugal.
1485	Felipa dies, and Columbus moves to Spain.
1486	Is denied support from King Ferdinand and Queen Isabella of Spain.
1491	Appeals again to Ferdinand and Isabella but is refused.
1492	King Ferdinand and Queen Isabella agree to finance Columbus's journey. On August 3, the *Niña*, the *Pinta*, and the *Santa María* set sail, heading west Lands in the New World on October 12.
1493	Returns to Spain on March 15, Embarks on his second journey to the New World on September 25.
1498	Begins his third voyage from Spain to the New World.
1500	Arrested and sent back to Spain in chains.
1502	Fourth and final voyage of Christopher Columbus.
1506	Dies on May 20 in Spain.

Timeline of the World

1271	Marco Polo travel overland from Europe to China.
1401	Competition in Florence for who will create the bronze doors for the baptistery of San Gionvanni.
1420	Jan van Eyck perfects the technique of oil painting.
1431	Joan of Arc is burned at the stake.
1433	China ends all oversea voyages and cuts itself off from foreign visitors.
1438	The Inca Empire in South America becomes the largest empire in the world.
1439	Johannes Gutenberg invents the printing press.
1453	The fall of Constantinople (present-day Istanbul) to the Ottoman Turks.
1487	Bartholomew Diaz sails around the southern tip of Africa.
1492	Ferdinand and Isabella expel all the Jews from Spain.
1497	Vasco da Gama sails to India.
1503	Leonardo da Vinci paints the *Mona Lisa.*
1506	Construction of St. Peter's Basilica in Rome begins.
1508	Michelangelo begins to paint the Sistine Chapel.

Blbliography

Bern, Emma Carlson. Christopher Columbus: The Voyage That Changed the World. Sterling Publishing Co., New York: 2008.

Columbus, Christopher. The Four Voyages of Christopher Columbus. trans. and ed. J.M. Cohen. Penguin Books, New York: 1969.

Doak, Robin S. Christopher Columbus: Explorer of the New World. Compass Point Books, Minneapolis: 2005.

Fritz, Jean. Where Do You Think You're Going, Christopher Columbus? G.P. Putnam's Sons, New York: 1980.

McNeese, Tim. Christopher Columbus and the Discovery of the Americas. Chelsea House, Philadelphia: 2006.

Roop, Peter, and Connie Roop. Christopher Columbus.In Their Own Words. Scholastic, New York: 2000.

Sundel, Al. Christopher Columbus and the Age of Exploration in World History. Enslow Publishers, Berkeley Heights, NJ: 2002.